AN
EASY ALBUM
FOR ORGAN

Soliloquy
HEALEY WILLAN

Minuet in Classical Style
C. ARMSTRONG GIBBS

Prelude
HENRY COLEMAN

In Green Pastures
HAROLD DARKE

Pastorale
SYDNEY WATSON

Finale in D minor
ERIC H. THIMAN

OXFORD UNIVERSITY PRESS
MUSIC DEPARTMENT
44 CONDUIT STREET, LONDON, W1R 0DE

AN EASY ALBUM

SOLILOQUY

HEALEY WILLAN

Printed in Great Britain

OXFORD UNIVERSITY PRESS, MUSIC DEPARTMENT, 44 CONDUIT STREET, LONDON, W1R 0DE

MINUET IN CLASSICAL STYLE

C. ARMSTRONG GIBBS

(Allargando 2nd time only)

Fine

D. C. al Fine

PRELUDE

HENRY COLEMAN

9

IN GREEN PASTURES

HAROLD DARKE

Allegretto e tranquillo

PASTORALE

SYDNEY WATSON

14

15

FINALE IN D MINOR

ERIC H. THIMAN

Moderato, con spirito (♩ = about 72 – 76)